Water Power

Focus: Energy

Meredith Costain

Water is used for many things. We drink water. We wash with water. We sometimes play with water.

Water can move things to make electricity. A waterfall can make electricity. Electricity made from falling water is called hydro-electricity.

Sometimes water from a dam is used to make electricity. The water in the dam flows through machines. The blades in the machines turn. The machines make electricity.

Long ago, river water was used to make flour. The water from the river flowed over a waterwheel. The spinning wheel turned the millstones. The millstones ground corn into flour.

Water that is boiled makes steam. Steam can make things move. Steam can make engines work. Long ago, ships had steam engines.

Trains also had steam engines. The steam pushed the train wheels to make them turn.

Paddle steamers had steam engines, too. The engines turned the wheels on the boats. The paddles on the wheels pushed against the water. This made the boat move.

COONAWARRA

Index